JARROLD SHORT WALKS
leisure walks for all ages

Sussex and South Downs

Compiled by
Brian Conduit

D1313468

JARROLD
publishing

Mapping
sourced from Ordnance Survey®

Text: Brian Conduit
Photography: Brian Conduit
Editors: Crawford Gillan, Sonya Calton
Designer: Doug Whitworth

© Jarrold Publishing 2003

OS Ordnance Survey® This product includes mapping data licensed from Ordnance Survey® with the permission of the Controller of Her Majesty's Stationery Office.
© Crown Copyright 2002. All rights reserved. Licence number 100017593. Ordnance Survey, the OS symbol and Pathfinder are registered trademarks and Explorer, Landranger and Outdoor Leisure are trademarks of the Ordnance Survey, the national mapping agency of Great Britain.

Jarrold Publishing ISBN 0-7117-2424-5

First published 2003
by Jarrold Publishing

Printed in Belgium
by Proost NV, Turnhout. 1/03

Jarrold Publishing
Pathfinder Guides, Whitefriars, Norwich NR3 1TR
E-mail: info@totalwalking.co.uk
www.totalwalking.co.uk

Front cover: Battle Abbey
Previous page: Signpost near Bignor Hill

Contents

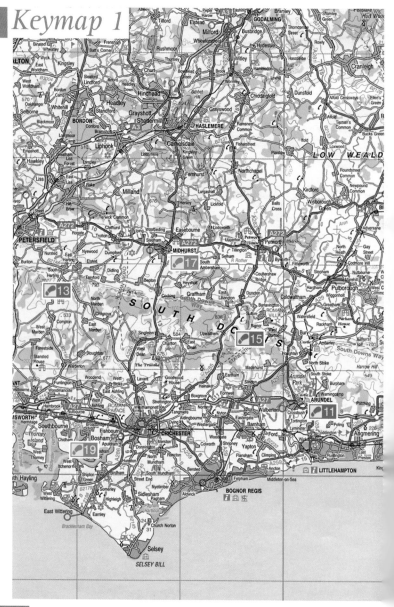

Keymap 1

SCALE 1:357 143 or 1 INCH to about 5¾ MILES *1CM to 3.5KM*

0   2   4   6   8   10 KILOMETRES   15

0   2   4   6   MILES 8   10

KEYMAP HEIGHTS SHOWN IN FEET

SCALE 1:357 143 or 1 INCH to about 5¾ MILES *1CM to 3.5KM*

0   2   4   6   8   10   KILOMETRES   15

0   2   4   6   MILES 8   10

KEYMAP HEIGHTS SHOWN IN FEET

⟂ Royal Sovereign

Introduction

Sussex is a county of contrasts and even contradictions. It has busy towns, busy roads and large holiday resorts. As it is relatively near London, it is a popular commuter area and Gatwick Airport lies within its borders. In complete contrast, it has isolated hamlets, extensive woodlands, open downs, lonely marshes and – in Ashdown Forest – the nearest that passes for a wilderness anywhere in south-east England. It also has attractive old market towns, picturesque villages, a wealth of historic attractions and excellent walking country.

The woodlands are remnants – sizeable ones – of the vast forest of the Weald or Andredesweald that covered much of the county in the Middle Ages. It is ironic that a commuter county, criss-crossed by main roads and railway lines and with an international airport, should in the past have been one of the most inaccessible parts of England, cut off from the rest of the country by these dense and almost impenetrable forests. This is the main reason why Sussex, the kingdom of the South Saxons – despite being next door to Kent, the first of the Anglo-Saxon kingdoms to receive Christianity – was the last to be converted.

Beachy Head

It is also ironic that a county that is now one of the most affluent in England should have been relatively poor in the Middle Ages. This is reflected in its medieval churches. Although there are many fine ones, and in particular some delightful small village churches, none of them can compare with those of the Cotswolds, the West Country, Lincolnshire or East Anglia. Even its greatest church, Chichester Cathedral, a superb example of Norman architecture and a most attractive building, does not rank in size and splendour with the cathedrals of York, Lincoln or Durham.

One other irony is that this region, nowadays much sought after because of its attractive towns and villages and largely unspoilt countryside, was once an industrial area. During the Middle Ages and up to the start of the Industrial Revolution, the Weald was a veritable 'Black Country', the centre of England's iron industry at the time.

Geography

The South Downs – described by Kipling as the 'blunt, bow-headed, whale-backed Downs' – are the most striking physical feature. These chalk downs sweep across the county from the Hampshire border to end at majestic Beachy Head, undoubtedly the best-known landmark in Sussex.

Here is to be found the most dramatic landscapes and the best walking country. On the escarpment of the downs, a series of viewpoints give extensive and memorable vistas across the Weald to the line of the North Downs and towards the coast. Although never rising to more than 800 ft (243m), some of the slopes of the downs are steep and provide quite energetic walking.

With two exceptions, the Sussex coast is mainly flat and, in many places, fairly built up. Those exceptions are where the South Downs end abruptly above the English Channel, producing not just Beachy Head but a whole succession of spectacular cliffs that includes the Seven Sisters and Seaford Head, and the sandstone cliffs to the east of Hastings, backed by a series of wooded glens and now a popular country park.

The lack of high cliffs does not mean that the rest of the coast is uninteresting. The creeks and inlets of Chichester Harbour and the reclaimed marshlands of Pevensey Bay and around Winchelsea and Rye have their own appeal and provide contrasting walking to the cliffs around Hastings and Beachy Head.

The Weald comprises the bulk of the county and lies between the South Downs and the North Downs in Kent and Surrey. Formerly thickly-forested, it is still a well-wooded area. It is also a complex and scenically varied area of sandstone and clay. The High Weald includes the elevated heathland of Ashdown Forest and the cliffs around Hastings. From these heights, grand views extend across the flatter, clay lands of the Low Weald, noted for villages of tile-hung houses and spacious greens and for its lazily meandering rivers.

Most of these rivers – Cuckmere, Ouse, Adur and Arun – flow north-south across the Weald, cut through the South Downs and then continue across the coastal lowlands to the English Channel. Delightful scenery is to be found in their valleys and riverside paths provide attractive and relaxing walking.

Towns and villages

Sussex has as fine a collection of handsome old towns as any county in England. Administratively, it is divided into two counties, West and East, and the respective county towns – Chichester, with its Norman cathedral, and Lewes, with its Norman castle – are two of the most interesting, with a varied range of buildings of all periods. In addition, there are the historic Cinque Ports of Rye and Winchelsea and the string of coastal resorts – Brighton, Hastings, Eastbourne – noted for their elegant terraces, squares and crescents dating from the Georgian, Regency and Victorian periods.

Villages are too numerous to mention individually but they range from small, flint hamlets tucked into folds of the downs, to the spacious villages of the Weald and the picturesque boating centres around Chichester Harbour.

Historic buildings

Chichester Cathedral is the most outstanding individual building but the multitude of historic sites includes prehistoric forts on the South Downs, the Roman villas at Fishbourne and Bignor, delightful village churches, timber-framed medieval manor houses and great country houses of the 17th and 18th centuries. In particular, the area is dotted with fortifications of all ages, built to protect this vulnerable stretch of coast and the approaches to the capital.

Near where William the Conqueror landed in 1066, there is a Roman fort which the Normans partly utilised as a castle and there are many other Norman and later castles. Among the most outstanding are the huge and much restored castle of the Dukes of Norfolk at Arundel, the

The ruins of Cowdray House

brick-built castle at Herstmonceux and the picture-postcard castle at Bodiam. Later defences include the Martello Towers and the Royal Military Canal, both constructed in the early 19th century in anticipation of a Napoleonic invasion.

Walking in Sussex

The main long distance route is the South Downs Way, one of the country's most popular national trails. In the main this follows the crest of the downs and links all the major viewpoints. Places associated with the Norman Conquest are linked by the 1066 Country Walk and other routes include the Downs Link, Sussex Border Path, Saxon Shore Way and Weald Way.

Sussex has a greater variety of landscapes and more tranquil and unspoilt walking areas than most other parts of south-east England. In general, waymarking of public rights of way is of a high standard. The main problems that walkers are likely to encounter – especially in parts of the Weald – are some muddy paths in the winter and overgrown paths in the summer. On the open downs, high winds can be a hazard and after wet weather, chalk can sometimes be sticky and awkward to walk on.

These problems are unlikely to spoil the enjoyment of a walk in any part of this delightful county, whatever the weather or season of the year.

1 Pevensey and Westham

START Pevensey, castle entrance

DISTANCE 2¼ miles (3.6km)

TIME 1½ hours

PARKING Pevensey

ROUTE FEATURES Flat walking across meadows, through a village and over marshland

The first part of the route, between the neighbouring villages of Pevensey and Westham, is across meadows by the walls of a Roman fort. You then enjoy a short and invigorating walk across the marshes of the Pevensey Levels and beside Pevensey Haven before returning to the start. There are wide and extensive views across the levels.

Facing the castle, turn left along a path that runs between the castle walls and Cattle Market car park. The path curves right to keep by the walls of the castle and Roman fort and then continues across meadows. After passing through trees and bushes, the path becomes fence-lined and enters Westham churchyard.

Keep to the left of the church, bear right in front of it and go through a gate onto a road. Turn left through the village of Westham, turn right along Peelings Lane, **A** passing to the right of a duck pond, continue

Pevensey Castle

PUBLIC TRANSPORT Buses and trains from Hastings, Bexhill and Eastbourne

REFRESHMENTS Pubs and café at Pevensey, pub at Westham

PUBLIC TOILETS Pevensey

ORDNANCE SURVEY MAPS Explorer 124 (Hastings & Bexhill), Landranger 199 (Eastbourne & Hastings)

along the lane and turn right along the tarmac track to Castle Farm. Climb a stile, continue along a track to enter a field and walk across it, over a low brow and down to a stile in the far right corner.

Climb it, veer slightly left across the next field and on the far side, cross a footbridge over a ditch. Bear right to climb a stile, head up steps, carefully cross the busy A27 and descend steps on the other side. Climb a stile and keep ahead across the meadows of the Pevensey Levels. Cross a ditch,

cross another one by waymarked gateposts, climb a stile by another ditch and walk across the next meadow, veering slightly right to a footpath post and footbridge over Pevensey Haven.

B Do not cross the bridge but turn right – here joining the 1066 Country Walk – and walk beside the haven. To the right, Westham church tower, the walls of Pevensey

> **?** *At Pevensey, the Normans built a castle within a Roman fort. Approximately how many years separate the two buildings?*

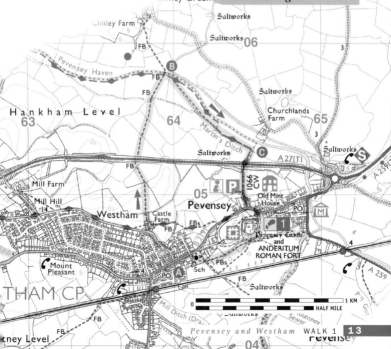

Pevensey Haven

Castle and the spire of Pevensey church can be seen.

C Turn right in the corner of the meadow, go through a gate, bear left to cross a ditch and continue along an enclosed path which bends right to a gate. Go through, almost immediately go through another one and recross the A27. Go through a gate, walk along an enclosed path and in front of the castle walls, turn left to return to the start. ●

Pevensey Castle is both a **Roman fort** and **Norman castle**. The Romans built the fort of Anderida in the late 3rd century. It was one of the 'Forts of the Saxon Shore', a defensive chain constructed along the south and east coasts of England to protect the coastline from Saxon raids. Most of the perimeter walls survive and make an impressive sight. Around the end of the 11th century, the Norman conquerors utilised the fort by building a castle in its south east corner. Although it subsequently became ruined, as late as World War II its defences were used as a machine gun post in the event of a German invasion.

The sturdy-looking church at **Westham** is one of the earliest Norman churches in the country. It was built in the late 11th century and extended and remodelled in the 14th and 15th centuries. It was the only church in the area until the one at Pevensey was founded in the early 13th century, a fine example of the **Early English** style of architecture. This meant that the people of Pevensey could worship without having to pass through the precincts of the castle.

Winchelsea and the Royal Military Canal

The walk across the marshes beside the Royal Military Canal is a bracing one and the views are wide and extensive. The canal runs along the base of the wooded cliff on which stands the village of Winchelsea, a fascinating place and well worth exploring.

From the centre of Winchelsea, walk along the road, passing to the right of St Thomas's Church. Continue along this road and just after it bends right, turn left over a stile Ⓐ. The wall on the left is all that remains of the medieval St John's Hospital.

Bear right downhill across a field to a stile. Climb it, do not climb the stile in front but turn left along an enclosed path to a lane. Turn right, follow this narrow lane around a right bend and pass through New Gate.

Winchelsea's ruined church

PUBLIC TRANSPORT Buses and trains from Hastings and Rye

REFRESHMENTS Pubs and café at Winchelsea

PUBLIC TOILETS Winchelsea

ORDNANCE SURVEY MAPS Explorer 124 (Hastings & Bexhill), Landranger 189 (Ashford & Romney Marsh)

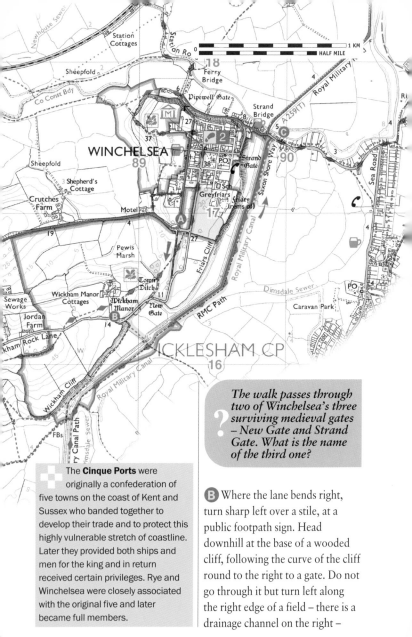

? The walk passes through two of Winchelsea's three surviving medieval gates – New Gate and Strand Gate. What is the name of the third one?

The **Cinque Ports** were originally a confederation of five towns on the coast of Kent and Sussex who banded together to develop their trade and to protect this highly vulnerable stretch of coastline. Later they provided both ships and men for the king and in return received certain privileges. Rye and Winchelsea were closely associated with the original five and later became full members.

B Where the lane bends right, turn sharp left over a stile, at a public footpath sign. Head downhill at the base of a wooded cliff, following the curve of the cliff round to the right to a gate. Do not go through it but turn left along the right edge of a field – there is a drainage channel on the right –

The Royal Military Canal

climb a stile, keep ahead and cross a footbridge over the Royal Military Canal. Turn left and follow a path beside it across marshes to a road.

C Turn left to recross the canal, keep ahead at a junction and take the first road on the left, signposted to Winchelsea. Head uphill, pass through Strand Gate and follow the road around a right bend to return to the start.

Winchelsea was built as a new town, commissioned by Edward I in the late 13th century after the old town was destroyed by storms and coastal erosion. It was conceived on a grand scale and was intended to be a major port for the French wine trade but it enjoyed only a brief heyday. Repeated attacks by the French during the Hundred Years' War and the receding sea led to its swift decline and it had ceased to be a port by the end of the 15th century. Now it is a quiet backwater, a fossilised town, and this is what gives it its fascination. Apart from the street pattern, a rare example of a planned medieval town, the main surviving monuments are three of the four original gateways, the 14th-century Court Hall (now a museum) and the ruined but imposing St Thomas's Church, comprising only the east end as the nave and transepts were destroyed by the French.

The Royal Military Canal was built in 1805 across the neck of the Dungeness peninsula as a defence against an anticipated invasion by **Napoleon**. It now makes an excellent walking route.

3

Barcombe Mills and the River Ouse

START Barcombe Mills, car park on minor road between Barcombe Cross and A26

DISTANCE 3 miles (4.8km)

TIME 1½ hours

PARKING Barcombe Mills

ROUTE FEATURES Disused railway track and riverside paths

The opening stretch is a pleasant, tree-lined walk along the track of a disused railway. The return is a delightful and relaxing stroll beside the River Ouse, ideal for a summer afternoon, and there are extensive views across the wide valley. A riverside pub with garden at the halfway point is an additional bonus.

The River Ouse

Take the path leading off from the car park which bends left to a track and turn right. Cross a succession of bridges over the various channels of the River Ouse – one of them is a former toll bridge – and follow the track around left and right bends to a crossways. Turn left along a tarmac track to a lane, keep ahead and after about 100 yds (91m), turn

? *How much did it cost to take a steam engine over the toll bridge crossed just after the start of the walk?*

PUBLIC TRANSPORT Infrequent buses from Lewes

REFRESHMENTS Pub at point **ⓒ**

PUBLIC TOILETS None

ORDNANCE SURVEY MAPS Explorer 122 (South Downs Way – Steyning to Newhaven), Landranger 198 (Brighton & Lewes)

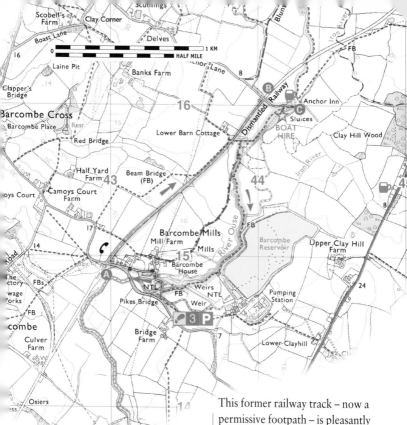

right along a track signposted to
Anchor Lane Ⓐ.

Part of the route uses the
track of a disused railway,
which opened in 1858 and closed in
the 1960s. It ran between **Lewes**
and **Uckfield** and served Barcombe
Mills. The former station buildings
have been converted into a private
residence.

This former railway track – now a
permissive footpath – is pleasantly
tree-lined and there are wide and
attractive views across the fields on
both sides. It later narrows to a
path and passes beside a gate onto
a narrow lane.

Ⓑ Turn right and where the lane
ends by the Anchor Inn, turn
right Ⓒ across grass beside the
river and climb a stile by a sluice.
Walk across riverside meadows and
then continue along an enclosed
path to a stile.

Climb it, keep ahead to a track, turn right and look out for where you turn left to cross a bridge over the river. Turn right to climb a stile and continue beside the Ouse. After climbing a stile, keep ahead along a tree-lined path beside water on both sides. Turn left to cross a footbridge, turn right to continue by the river and below the embankment of Barcombe Reservoir on the left and soon after climbing a stile, bear slightly left away from the Ouse. Cross another footbridge, bear right beside the river again and climb a stile.

It is difficult to believe that the tranquil surroundings at the start of the walk were once a busy industrial site. There has been a flour mill at **Barcombe Mills** since the Middle Ages but the most recent building, erected in 1870, was burnt down in 1939 and little of it remains. Now the area around it is popular with walkers and anglers.

Keep ahead along a path, go up steps and go through a squeezer stile onto a track. Turn left, here picking up the outward route, and retrace your steps to the start of the walk. ●

Former railway trackbed at Barcombe Mills

Alfriston, Litlington and the River Cuckmere

START Alfriston

DISTANCE 3 miles (4.8km)

TIME 1½ hours

PARKING Alfriston

ROUTE FEATURES Most of the route is along a lane and across riverside meadows

4

The walk starts by crossing the River Cuckmere to the isolated and tiny Lullington church and continues along a quiet road into the village of Litlington. After recrossing the Cuckmere, the return leg is a relaxing stroll across attractive riverside meadows.

The walk begins at the Market Cross in the centre of Alfriston. Facing down the village street, turn left along a lane – there are South Downs Way and No Through Road signs – and at a

Riverside meadows near Alfriston

T-junction, turn right along a track towards the church.

Ⓐ At the next T-junction, turn left along a tarmac path and cross a bridge over the River Cuckmere. Continue along an enclosed path to a road in front of Great Meadow Barn. Turn right and immediately turn left, at a public footpath sign to Jevington and Lullington church. Walk up steps and continue

? *In which year was Great Meadow Barn – passed between Alfriston and Lullington church – built?*

PUBLIC TRANSPORT Buses from Lewes, Eastbourne and Seaford

REFRESHMENTS Pubs and cafés at Alfriston, pub and tearoom at Litlington

PUBLIC TOILETS Alfriston

ORDNANCE SURVEY MAPS Explorer 123 (South Downs Way – Newhaven to Eastbourne), Landranger 199 (Eastbourne & Hastings)

along an enclosed path, later heading gently uphill along the left edge of a field and following signs to Lullington church all the time. Look out for where the path veers left to a stile, climb it and continue along a tree-lined path between embankments to a road. Before reaching the road, a brief detour along a path on the left leads to the church.

B Turn right along the road and follow it for almost 1 mile (1.6km) into Litlington, passing to the left of the Norman church.

C Just before reaching the pub, turn right, at a public footpath sign, along an enclosed tarmac path, go

> The isolated **Lullington church**, half-hidden by trees, claims to be one of the smallest churches in the country. In fact it is only half a church, the chancel of a larger church whose nave was destroyed. It dates mainly from the 13th century.

Alfriston

through a belt of trees and at a footpath post, follow the path to the left and turn right to cross a bridge over the Cuckmere. Immediately turn right, at a public footpath sign, along an enclosed path **D** and go through a kissing-gate. Now comes a most pleasant and relaxing finale to the walk as you continue across meadows beside the meandering river, going through a series of kissing-gates. There are attractive views across the valley and the spire of Alfriston church is in sight for much of the way. Eventually, you pass to the right of the church to reach the footbridge crossed previously **A**. From here retrace your steps to the start. ●

Until the 18th century **Alfriston** was a port and its comparative isolation, just upriver from a lonely stretch of coast, made it an ideal smuggling centre. It is one of the most appealing villages in Sussex, attractively situated below the downs and on the banks of the River Cuckmere. Its main street is lined with old houses, shops, tearooms and medieval inns and across an open grassy area called the Tye stands the imposing, 14th-century, cruciform church, the '**Cathedral of the Downs**', overlooking riverside meadows. By the church is the thatched, timber-framed, Clergy House, built around the same time. It was the first building acquired by the recently-formed National Trust in 1896.

5 Bodiam Castle and the Rother Valley

There are short stretches beside the River Rother, pleasant woodland and fine views over the valley. These views are inevitably dominated by Bodiam Castle, an outstanding and highly photogenic building.

START Bodiam Castle, National Trust car park

DISTANCE 3½ miles (5.6km)

TIME 2 hours

PARKING Bodiam Castle

ROUTE FEATURES Easy walking mostly along field and woodland paths, some may become muddy after rain and be overgrown in the summer

? Who was the builder of Bodiam Castle?

Turn left out of the car park, cross the bridge over the River Rother and turn left over a stile a few yards ahead **A**. Turn left again, climb an embankment and bear right along it above the river.

In front of a gate, turn right to descend from the embankment, walk along the left edge of a field, by a drainage channel on the left, and turn right in the corner to continue along the field edge. Look out for where you turn left over a stile, cross a railway line, climb a stile opposite and turn left to immediately climb another one. Turn right, passing to the right of a barn, cross a footbridge, keep ahead by the right edge of a field and cross another footbridge in the corner **B**.

Bear left across a field to a stile, climb it and continue uphill across the next field, making for a stile in the left corner. After climbing it, walk along the left field edge, turn left over a stile, keep ahead through a belt of trees to go

PUBLIC TRANSPORT Buses between Hastings and Tunbridge Wells

REFRESHMENTS Pubs at Bodiam and Ewhurst Green, tearoom at Bodiam Castle

PUBLIC TOILETS At start

ORDNANCE SURVEY MAPS Explorer 136 (The Weald), Landranger 199 (Eastbourne & Hastings)

through a kissing-gate and turn right to continue uphill along the right edge of a field. Go through a gate onto a lane on the edge of Ewhurst Green – pub and church are to the left – and turn right **C**. At a T-junction, keep ahead **D** over a stile, follow a path across a field towards woodland and climb a stile in the right corner to enter the wood.

This is Smutts Wood, an ancient woodland. Continue through it, cross a footbridge and keep ahead

The railway line crossed soon after the start of the walk is the **Kent and East Sussex Railway**, first opened in 1900 and closed down in 1961. Through the work of volunteers, it was later partially re-opened and steam trains now run along an 11-mile length between Bodiam and Tenterden.

through a traditional orchard to emerge onto a track at a bend.

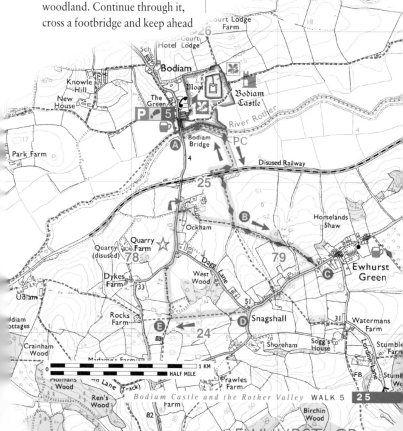

E Turn right along a grassy path (still through the orchard), climb a stile and keep ahead along a narrow path between pools to a stile. Climb it, bear left to climb another one and walk along the left edge of a field, by a line of trees on the left. Climb a stile, keep ahead, go through a gate, turn right along a track and go through another gate onto a road. Turn right downhill and, opposite the entrance to Quarry Farm, turn right, at a public footpath stone, along an enclosed tarmac track.

After a slight left bend, turn right over a waymarked stile and walk diagonally across a field to climb another stile. Keep in the same direction across the next field, climb a stile, head downhill along the left field edge and in the corner, go through a hedge gap.

B Turn left along the left edge of a field, here picking up the outward route, and retrace your steps to the start. ●

With its walls, towers and gatehouse rising above the waters of the moat, **Bodiam** is everyone's idea of what a medieval castle should look like and is therefore a popular subject for calendars and birthday cards. It is one of the later medieval castles, built in the late-14th century to protect the Rother valley from possible French raids. It was never attacked by the French and saw very little action. After falling into ruin, it was bought by **Lord Curzon** in 1916 who restored it and later gave it to the National Trust.

Bodiam Castle

Seven Sisters and Cuckmere Haven

The walk does not go over the chalk cliffs of the Seven Sisters but provides the most memorable views of them as you descend from Short Cliff into Cuckmere Haven. You continue along the side of the haven above the river – which does a number of loops – before heading gently uphill back to the start. The magnificent coastal views extend from Seaford Bay to Beachy Head.

6

START South Hill Barn car park, take Sutton Road on east side of Seaford, turn along Chyngton Road and where it ends, turn right along concrete track up to car park
DISTANCE 3¼ miles (5.2km)
TIME 1½ hours
PARKING South Hill Barn
ROUTE FEATURES A combination of clifftop, downland and walking along an embankment above Cuckmere Haven

Start by taking the concrete track to the left of the barn and pass beside a barrier to a three-way fork. Take the middle track and just in front of a cattle-grid, bear right along a grassy path which heads gently down through Hope Bottom to the sea.

Cliffs near Seaford

Despite their name, the **Seven Sisters** are actually a series of eight chalk cliffs between Beachy Head to the east and Cuckmere Haven to the west. They form one of the most spectacular stretches of coastline in England and are seen at their best on the descent into Cuckmere Haven from Seaford.

PUBLIC TRANSPORT None
REFRESHMENTS None
PUBLIC TOILETS None
ORDNANCE SURVEY MAPS Explorer 123 (South Downs Way – Newhaven to Eastbourne), Landranger 199 (Eastbourne & Hastings)

Cuckmere Haven, the beautiful and unspoilt estuary of the River Cuckmere, comprises a mixture of shingle beach and lagoon. The river does a series of large loops on the final stage of its journey to the sea and its mouth is almost blocked by a bar of sand and shingle. In 1846 a straight channel was dug to reduce flooding.

A At a fork, take the left-hand uphill path onto the clifftop and bear left to continue over Short Cliff. The views ahead of the Seven Sisters, Beachy Head and Cuckmere Haven are magnificent. On reaching a track, bear right downhill, passing to the left of cottages, go through a gate and

97

Seven Sisters

keep ahead along a shingle embankment across Cuckmere Haven to the river.

B Turn left and continue along another embankment above the Cuckmere, finally going around a left bend to a crossways **C**.

Keep ahead through a waymarked gate, head gently uphill along the right edge of a field, go through a gate in the corner and turn left along an enclosed track. Take the first path on the right (also enclosed), go through a belt of trees to a T-junction and turn left along a track, **D** passing in front of houses. Pass beside a barrier, keep ahead to join a concrete track and follow it uphill back to the start.

●

> **?** What word is used to describe the large loops in the river at Cuckmere Haven?

7 Bramber and the Adur Valley

START Bramber
DISTANCE 3½ miles (5.6km)
TIME 2 hours
PARKING Bramber
ROUTE FEATURES Mainly field and riverside walking

Three ancient churches, including a Saxon one, plus a ruined medieval castle indicate that a lot of historic interest is packed into this short and easy walk. At this point the River Adur carves a gap through the South Downs on its way to the sea and about half the route is beside the river.

Turn right out of the car park along the road through the village and turn right again into Castle Lane. *A brief detour to the right enables you to visit Bramber Castle and church.* Continue along the lane and at a public footpath sign, turn right along a track through woodland.

At the next public footpath sign, bear left, continue through the trees to a stile, climb it and keep ahead along an embankment, curving slightly left to another stile.

A After climbing it, turn right,

Although **Bramber** is now a quiet and picturesque backwater, it was once an important river port with a great Norman castle. It declined from the 14th century onwards because the river receded and became too shallow. Only fragments of the keep and outer walls remain of the castle, built by **William de Braose**, a follower of William the Conqueror, in the late 11th century. He also built the church at the same time, which served as the castle chapel as well as the local parish church. Although it retains some of its early Norman work, the church was badly damaged during the Parliamentary siege of the castle in the Civil War and was rebuilt and restored in the 18th and 19th centuries.

PUBLIC TRANSPORT Buses from Pulborough and Henfield
REFRESHMENTS Pubs at Bramber and at Upper Beeding
PUBLIC TOILETS Bramber
ORDNANCE SURVEY MAPS Explorer 122 (South Downs Way – Steyning to Newhaven), Landranger 198 (Brighton & Lewes)

continue across the field, cross a bridge over the River Adur and turn right along another embankment above it. *For a brief detour to visit the church at Upper Beeding, descend the embankment where the river curves right,* **B**

walk across a meadow, cross a footbridge over a channel, climb steps and the church is just ahead.

Retrace your steps to the embankment **B** and continue along it – there are stiles and gates

– to emerge onto a road at Beeding Bridge. Turn right over the footbridge beside it, turn left down steps,  walk along a path, climb steps and then a stile and continue beside the river again, climbing more stiles. Go under a modern road bridge and at a T-junction where the river bends left, turn right onto a clear

Bramber - village, church and castle

and well-surfaced path to a finger-post. **D**

For another brief detour – to the Saxon church at Botolphs – keep ahead, pass beside a gate onto a lane and turn left. Return to the finger-post, **D** turn left and walk along an enclosed path. Bramber Castle and church can be seen ahead.

E Follow the path around a right bend above a channel, turn left over a stile and carefully cross the busy A283. Keep ahead to climb a stile and at a fork immediately

Botolphs church

Brief diversions on the walk enable you to see two interesting old churches. The mainly 13th-century church at **Upper Beeding** was once the church of Sele Priory, founded by William of Braose and served by Benedictine monks from Normandy.

The isolated church at Botolphs is of Saxon origin and retains some of its original Saxon architecture, particularly the chancel arch. The village of Botolphs was an outpost of the port of Bramber and there was once a bridge over the Adur here, thought to have been originally constructed by the Romans as part of the '**tin road**' that linked the tin mines of Cornwall with the port of Pevensey. The receding river destroyed the port and the village became deserted.

ahead, take the left-hand path across a field and climb a stile on the far side.

Turn right along an enclosed path, turn left to continue along a track and climb a stile between two gates. Keep ahead to a footpath post, climb a stile and continue along a tree-lined, tarmac track to a road in Bramber. Turn left, passing St Mary's House, a picturesque, half-timbered, late medieval building, to return to the start. ●

Why does Botolphs church stand on its own?

8 Herstmonceux – Castle and Church

START Windmill Hill
DISTANCE 3½ miles (5.6km)
TIME 1½ hours
PARKING Roadside parking at Windmill Hill
ROUTE FEATURES The start and finish is along a tarmac track, much of the rest is through or beside woodland

There is pleasant walking across fields and through woodland on this undemanding walk. There are also fine views over rolling countryside and the two focal points are the adjacent medieval castle and church at Herstmonceux, both nearly 2 miles (3.2km) from the village.

The walk starts in front of the Horseshoe Inn. Facing the inn, turn right along a hedge- and tree-lined tarmac track (Comphurst Lane).

A After almost ½ mile (800m), turn left, at a public footpath sign, along a track to a gate. Go through, walk across a field – one of the domes of the former Royal Observatory can be seen ahead – go through another gate, keep in the same direction across the next field and go through a gate on the far side.

Continue along an enclosed path into woodland, keep by the left inside edge of the trees and soon after passing a pool on the left – where the path starts to descend – you reach a fork. Take the right-hand path which heads uphill through Plantation Wood, by a wire fence on the right, and climb a stile to emerge from the trees. Continue in the same direction across a field – more observatory domes are to the right – and in the far right corner, keep ahead through a belt of trees and climb a stile onto a road.

Turn right and just past the entrance to Herstmonceux Castle

PUBLIC TRANSPORT Buses from Eastbourne, Bexhill and Hastings
REFRESHMENTS Pub at Windmill Hill
PUBLIC TOILETS None
ORDNANCE SURVEY MAPS Explorer 124 (Hastings & Bexhill), Landranger 199 (Eastbourne & Hastings)

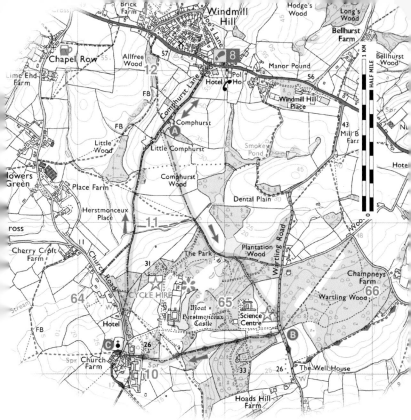

and Science Centre, turn right, **B** at a public bridleway sign to Herstmonceux church, along a path which keeps by the right inside edge of woodland. Head downhill, passing through several gates, and continue across a field to a crossways and finger-post. From here there is a fine view of the castle to the right, and an even better one if you turn right and walk across the field for a short distance.

The route keeps ahead to a gate on the far side of the field. Go through, continue through trees to go through another one and keep ahead between some of the Science Centre buildings. After going through another gate onto a track, continue to Herstmonceux church and turn right along a lane. **C**

> ? *Why does a Canadian flag fly from the gatehouse of Herstmonceux Castle?*

Herstmonceux Castle

At a public bridleway sign, bear right along a path through trees, keep ahead at a finger-post and after going through a gate, there is a superb view ahead over rolling country, including the large house of Herstmonceux Place and the village of Windmill Hill.

Veer slightly right and head downhill across a field. At the bottom, continue along a short stretch of enclosed track and then head uphill along the left edge of a field to a gate. Go through, keep ahead to enter woodland, walk along its left inside edge and continue along an enclosed track which emerges onto a tarmac track. This is Comphurst Lane and you follow it back to the start. ●

Herstmonceux church is near the castle and about 2 miles (3.2km) from Herstmonceux village. This picturesque building dates mainly from the 13th and 14th centuries and is unusual in that the tower is above the north side of the nave. Inside are monuments to the Fiennes family who owned the castle.

With its brick walls and towers rising above the moat, **Herstmonceux Castle** is a most impressive sight. It was built in the 15th century by Sir Roger Fiennes and is one of the earliest brick-built structures in the country. Despite its moat and battlements, it was built for comfort rather than defence – like many other late medieval castles – and saw little action. After falling into ruin and being partially dismantled, it was restored in the early-20th century and from 1946 to 1988, it was the home of the **Royal Observatory**, hence the domes. The grounds and gardens are open to the public and there is a Science Centre on the site.

Warren and Fairlight Glens

START Hastings Country Park, Coastguard Lane car park, by Fairlight church

DISTANCE 3½ miles (5.6km)

TIME 2 hours

PARKING Hastings Country Park

ROUTE FEATURES Some quite steep ascents and descents along cliffs and through coastal woodland

Hastings Country Park comprises the stretch of spectacular coastline to the east of the town and the walk takes you through two of the wooded glens that cut into the cliffs. As well as attractive woodland, there are superb views along the coast. The several steep ascents and descents are made easier by steps and route finding is aided by numbered bollards.

Walk along the tarmac path at the side of the car park to a lane and turn right. Where the lane ends at the country park visitor centre, keep ahead beside another car park and along a tarmac track, passing to the left of a row of coastguards' cottages. Ⓐ

Where the track bends left, keep ahead through a kissing-gate, continue downhill towards the sea and at a footpath post, turn right along a path to a kissing-gate. Go through, keep ahead and descend through fern and gorse, via steps in places, into Warren Glen. At a footpath post, turn left down a flight of steps, continue along a

Fairlight church

PUBLIC TRANSPORT Buses from Hastings, Rye and Winchelsea

REFRESHMENTS Café at start

PUBLIC TOILETS At start

ORDNANCE SURVEY MAPS Explorer 124 (Hastings & Bexhill), Landranger 199 (Eastbourne & Hastings)

Hastings Country Park
comprises 650 acres (260 ha) of coastline to the east of the town, stretching from East Cliff to Fairlight. There are superb views from the cliffs, westwards over Hastings and across Pevensey Bay and eastwards across Rye Bay. The series of steep-sided, thickly-wooded glens – Ecclesbourne, Fairlight and Warren – that cut into the cliffs provide attractive and quite energetic walking. The Old Town and Norman castle at Hastings are well worth a visit.

winding path through trees and gorse and after crossing a stream, head steeply uphill to a footpath post. Continue beyond it to bollard 13, head uphill through woodland (more steps) and at the top, keep ahead across an open area, by a wire fence on the right.

Descend steps again through more woodland and at a T-junction by

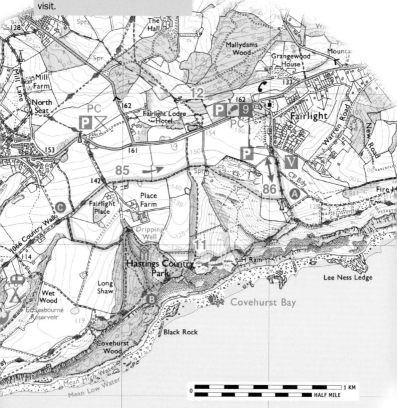

A distant view of the coast near Fairlight

bollard 11, turn left and continue down, following the curving path into Fairlight Glen.

B At a junction of paths by bollard 10, turn right, in the Upper Fairlight Glen and Barley Lane direction, climbing steadily above the glen to a junction by bollard 9. Turn sharp left, passing to the right of the bollard, along an uphill track which soon levels off, emerges from the trees and curves right to continue up to a stile at a crossways. Climb it and keep ahead, in the Barley Lane direction, along a hedge-lined track which bends right to a track.

C Turn right to a T-junction, keep ahead through a kissing-gate, at a public footpath sign to Warren Glen and Fire Hills, and walk along a narrow enclosed path to a stile. After climbing it, continue along the left edge of a field, pass through a gap, keep along the right edge of the next field and go through a kissing-gate onto a track.

Cross over, bear right along a grassy track and at a fork, take the right-hand path (despite the direction of a waymark) which heads up between gorse and fern to redundant gateposts. Go through, walk across a field to a tarmac track to the left of the coastguards' cottages and turn left **A** to return to the start. ●

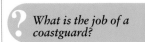
What is the job of a coastguard?

10 *Ardingly Reservoir and Village*

START Ardingly Reservoir, car park signposted from B2028 on edge of Ardingly

DISTANCE 4 miles (6.4km)

TIME 2 hours

PARKING Ardingly Reservoir

ROUTE FEATURES Easy walking across fields, through woodland and beside a reservoir

After a beautiful opening stretch along the wooded shores of the reservoir, the route continues through woodland and along a lane into Ardingly village. On the second half of the walk, mainly along field paths and tracks and through more woodland, there are fine views over the Weald and you pass through the buildings of Ardingly College.

Start in front of the information board and turn right to join a path just beyond a public footpath sign. The path initially keeps along the left edge of woodland, later continues beside Ardingly Reservoir and eventually winds up through woodland to go through a kissing-gate onto a lane.

Ⓐ Turn right uphill and at a

? *The maximum capacity of Ardingly Reservoir is equivalent to how many cans of Coke?*

public footpath sign, bear right along a path and descend steps through woodland. At a fork just beyond a plank footbridge, take the left-hand path steeply uphill and at the top, curve left and continue along an enclosed path to a lane.

Ⓑ Turn left and at a T-junction by Ardingly church, turn right along a lane into the village. At a road junction in the village centre, keep ahead, in the Lindfield and Haywards Heath direction, and at a public footpath sign, turn right

PUBLIC TRANSPORT Infrequent buses from East Grinstead and Haywards Heath to Ardingly village

REFRESHMENTS Pubs and café at Ardingly

PUBLIC TOILETS None

ORDNANCE SURVEY MAPS Explorer 135 (Ashdown Forest), Landranger 198 (Brighton & Lewes)

C along a tarmac track between houses which curves right to another footpath sign. Turn left along a tree-lined path to a stile, climb it and keep ahead along the left edge of a field. In front is a fine view over the Weald to the line of

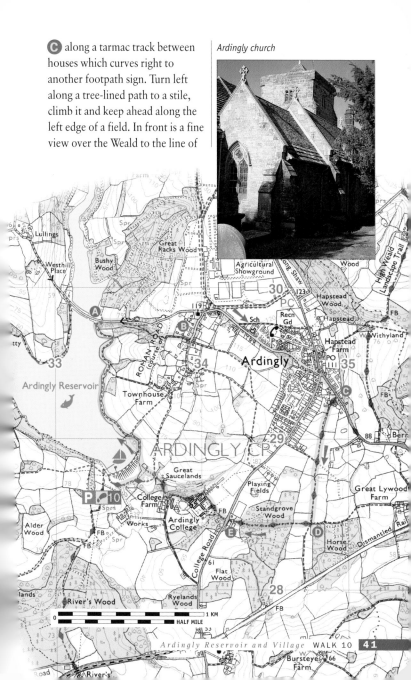

Ardingly church

the South Downs. Climb a stile, head gently downhill across the next field to a finger-post and continue beyond it, crossing a concrete track, to a gate. Go through, follow a worn path across a field, pass through a hedge gap, keep along the left edge of the next field.

D At another finger-post about halfway along it, turn right and head across the field towards woodland.

Climb a stile, continue through the delightful Standgrove Wood and on emerging from the trees, keep ahead along a track to a road.

E Cross over and walk along the tarmac drive of Ardingly College, passing to the right of the main buildings. The drive bends left between school buildings and then bears right and heads downhill.

Ardingly Reservoir was formed by damming two small tributaries of the River Ouse. It was constructed in the 1970s and, when full, is 45 ft (14m) deep and can hold around 5000 million gallons of water. Much of its shoreline is well-wooded and this, together with its irregular shape, gives it a more natural appearance than many reservoirs.

Ardingly's attractive church, about ½ mile (800m) to the west of the village centre, was built mainly in the 14th and 15th centuries. The red-brick buildings of **Ardingly College** are situated to the south of the village and the latter part of the route passes between some of them. The college was founded in 1858 and opened in 1870.

At a finger-post by a fork, continue downhill along the right-hand track – there is a pool on the right – follow it around a left bend and at another finger-post just before reaching a gate, turn left along a path through trees and bushes. Climb a stile and turn left to return to the start. ●

The Weald near Ardingly

Arundel Park and the River Arun

START	Arundel
DISTANCE	4 miles (6.4km)
TIME	2 hours
PARKING	Arundel
ROUTE FEATURES	Open and hilly parkland, followed by wooded lakeshore and flat riverside walking

11

An opening uphill stretch leads from the town centre into Arundel Park. There are superb views as you descend into a dry valley and this is followed by beautiful woodland walking beside Swanbourne Lake. On the final leg, you keep along an embankment which follows the River Arun around a right bend, enjoying magnificent views of the skyline of Arundel, dominated by the castle, church and Roman Catholic cathedral. Note that dogs are not allowed in Arundel Park.

Start in High Street by the war memorial and walk up the street, curving left alongside the castle walls. Pass to the left of the parish church and to the right of the Roman Catholic cathedral and at a public footpath sign, turn right along a tarmac track to enter Arundel Park **A**.

Go through a kissing-gate by a lodge and head gently uphill, keeping along the main tarmac track all the while.

B At a waymarked post in front of the Hiorne Tower (built in 1790), turn right and walk across grass to another waymarked post. Cross a gallop, continue downhill by the left edge of trees to a track and turn left over a stile. Continue along the track – there are superb views ahead up a steep-sided, dry valley – which descends through trees to a crossways in the valley bottom **C**.

? *From which century do the ruins of the Dominican friary, passed near the end of the walk, date?*

PUBLIC TRANSPORT Buses from Worthing, Brighton, Amberley and Chichester; trains from Littlehampton, Chichester and Pulborough
REFRESHMENTS Pubs and cafés at Arundel, café by Swanbourne Lake
PUBLIC TOILETS Arundel
ORDNANCE SURVEY MAPS Explorer 121 (Arundel & Pulborough), Landranger 197 (Chichester & the South Downs)

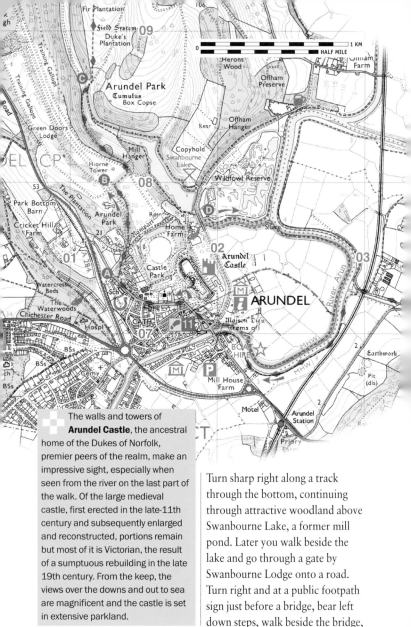

The walls and towers of **Arundel Castle**, the ancestral home of the Dukes of Norfolk, premier peers of the realm, make an impressive sight, especially when seen from the river on the last part of the walk. Of the large medieval castle, first erected in the late-11th century and subsequently enlarged and reconstructed, portions remain but most of it is Victorian, the result of a sumptuous rebuilding in the late 19th century. From the keep, the views over the downs and out to sea are magnificent and the castle is set in extensive parkland.

Turn sharp right along a track through the bottom, continuing through attractive woodland above Swanbourne Lake, a former mill pond. Later you walk beside the lake and go through a gate by Swanbourne Lodge onto a road. Turn right and at a public footpath sign just before a bridge, bear left down steps, walk beside the bridge, climb some steps and walk across Swanbourne Footbridge.

D Immediately, at a waymarked post, turn left along a tree-lined path by a stream to the River Arun.

After climbing a stile, turn right onto an embankment above the river and follow the Arun around a large right curve, going through several kissing-gates and enjoying the superb and ever-changing views of the castle, church and cathedral at Arundel.

On approaching the town, bear right down the embankment and walk across a car park to a road. Turn left, passing the remains of a medieval Dominican friary, to the bridge and turn right along High Street to the start.

Arundel is situated on a spur of the South Downs and from the castle, church and cathedral, the streets descend steeply to the bridge over the River Arun. The two major ecclesiastical buildings in the town symbolise the somewhat uneasy relationship that existed after the Reformation between the mainly Protestant townsfolk and the Catholic Dukes of Norfolk, owners of the castle. The 14th-century church is unique in that the nave is Anglican and the east end – **the Fitzalan Chapel** – Catholic and for a long time the two halves were walled off from each other. Now, in these more ecumenical times, they are separated by a glass screen that can be opened when necessary. After the Catholic church was allowed to organise itself into dioceses again, the building of the imposing Roman Catholic cathedral was financed by the 15th **Duke of Norfolk** in the 1870s. It is built in the French Gothic style.

Arundel Castle

12 *Chanctonbury Ring*

The route heads up onto the South Downs and continues to the prehistoric fort of Chanctonbury Ring. The extensive views from here across the rolling downland include the earthworks of Cissbury Ring, another prehistoric site. Both at the start and on the final descent, you pass through attractive woodland.

START Chanctonbury Picnic Site, off A283 to the east of Washington

DISTANCE 4 miles (6.4km)

TIME 2 hours

PARKING Chanctonbury Picnic Site

ROUTE FEATURES Woodland and downland walking, some climbing but not particularly taxing

Start by turning left out of the car park along a tarmac track and at a public bridleway sign, turn right along an enclosed track **A**. At a fork, take the left-hand track through woodland which climbs gently to a gate. Go through, keep ahead along the right edge of woodland, curving first left and then right, go through another gate and continue up – later by the right inside edge of trees again – to a junction and footpath post.

Continue gently uphill, bearing left, and at a fork, take the right-

At 780 ft (238m), the Iron Age fort of **Chanctonbury Ring** is situated at one of the highest points on the South Downs and commands extensive views. In clear weather, there is a magnifcent view looking southwards across the wide and empty expanses of the downs towards the larger fort of **Cissbury Ring** and the coast. The circle of trees that crowns the fort, planted in the 1760s by Charles Goring, a local landowner, was badly damaged during the great gale that swept over south eastern England in the autumn of 1987.

hand path – there is a blue-waymarked post here – which

PUBLIC TRANSPORT Buses from Pulborough and Steyning run along the A283 about 1 mile (1.6km) north of the picnic site

REFRESHMENTS None

PUBLIC TOILETS None

ORDNANCE SURVEY MAPS Explorer 121 (Arundel & Pulborough), Landranger 198 (Brighton & Lewes)

finally emerges from the trees. Keep ahead across grassland to a T-junction and turn sharp left, **B** here joining the South Downs Way. Head uphill to another T-junction, turn left **C** and continue gently uphill, passing to the right of a triangulation pillar, to reach

Chanctonbury Ring. The track continues past it, curving right to a stile, climb it and keep ahead.

> **?** *What type of trees crown Chanctonbury Ring?*

D At a footpath post, turn left along a path which enters woodland. The path descends through Chalkpit Wood, bends sharply to the right and continues down by the left inside edge of the trees. Go through a gate and keep ahead to the start. ●

Chanctonbury Ring

Harting Down

START Harting Down, National Trust car park, on B2141 about 1 mile (1.6km) to the south of South Harting

DISTANCE 3½ miles (5.6km)

TIME 2 hours

PARKING Harting Down

ROUTE FEATURES Across downland and through woodland, with one steep ascent and descent

This exhilarating walk takes you along the crest of the South Downs to the 794-ft (242m) summit of Beacon Hill, site of an Iron Age fort and the highest point on the downs. The magnificent views from here extend along the downs and over both the coast and the Weald. The return leg is a pleasant walk across fields and through woodland.

Right from the start, you enjoy a superb view from the crest of the downs looking over the Weald. Begin by heading across to a South Downs Way post and turn right to a gate. Go through and keep ahead along a path which later becomes enclosed and descends into Bramshott Bottom.

The route now heads steeply up the flanks of Beacon Hill to a gate. After going through it, continue more gently up and at a fork, take the right-hand path to reach the triangulation pillar and view indicator at the top. From here –

the highest point on the South Downs – the extensive and magnificent views take in downs, coast and Weald. Continue past the triangulation pillar, heading steeply downhill to the base of the hill, and turn sharp right along a track.

A The track contours across the hillside and at a T-junction just after entering trees, turn right, **B** go through a gate and keep ahead.

At a footpath post, turn left **C** – here leaving the South Downs Way – along a grassy path that descends gently to a crossways. Keep ahead,

PUBLIC TRANSPORT Very occasional buses from Petersfield and Chichester

REFRESHMENTS None

PUBLIC TOILETS None

ORDNANCE SURVEY MAPS Explorer 120 (Chichester), Landranger 197 (Chichester & the South Downs)

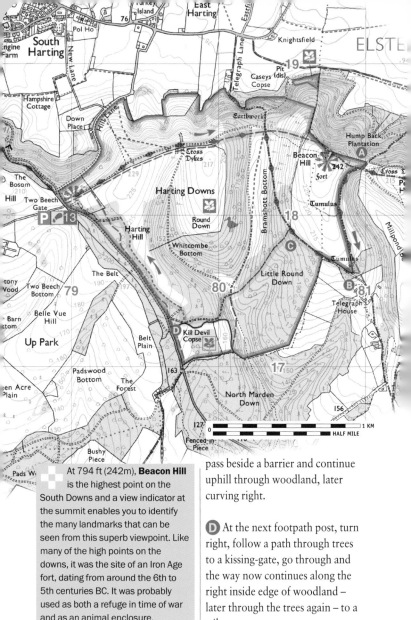

At 794 ft (242m), **Beacon Hill** is the highest point on the South Downs and a view indicator at the summit enables you to identify the many landmarks that can be seen from this superb viewpoint. Like many of the high points on the downs, it was the site of an Iron Age fort, dating from around the 6th to 5th centuries BC. It was probably used as both a refuge in time of war and as an animal enclosure.

pass beside a barrier and continue uphill through woodland, later curving right.

D At the next footpath post, turn right, follow a path through trees to a kissing-gate, go through and the way now continues along the right inside edge of woodland – later through the trees again – to a stile.

The South Downs Way is one of Britain's most popular and scenic national trails. It runs for approximately 106 miles (171km) from Eastbourne to Winchester, mainly following the ridge of the rolling downs, and there are a series of magnificent viewpoints. Although the walking is generally easy and the downs never exceed 800 ft (243m) in height, some of the climbs onto the escarpment are quite steep and exhausting.

Climb it and head gently uphill along the left edge of a field, by woodland on the left, curving left to a gate. Turn left through it and walk across the grass to the car park.

●

? *At the start of the walk, what is the name of the village seen below at the foot of the South Downs?*

The view over The Weald from Harting Down

14 *Ditchling Beacon*

START Ditchling Beacon,
National Trust car park
DISTANCE 4½ miles
(7.2km)
TIME 2 hours
PARKING Ditchling
Beacon
ROUTE FEATURES Easy
walking mostly over open
downland, with gentle
gradients

*From the superb viewpoint of Ditchling
Beacon, you head gently downhill into
North Bottom and continue through this
fine, dry chalk valley. A gentle ascent to
rejoin the South Downs Way is followed by
an exhilarating walk along the crest of the
downs, with more magnificent views.*

Start by the Ditchling Beacon
information board and turn left
along a track, part of the South
Downs Way, to a gate. Go through,
keep ahead over the beacon and
the triangulation pillar on the
highest point can be reached by a
brief detour to the left.

A At a footpath post, turn left
through a gate, here leaving the
South Downs Way. As you walk
along a path across fields, there are
wonderful views over rolling
downland. Go through a gate, keep
ahead and the track descends to
another gate and a public

bridleway
sign. Go
through the
gate to a fork,
take the right-
hand path which
continues down
into North
Bottom, curving
right to a gate, go
through and continue through the
bottom of this dry valley. At
waymark 38, turn right through a
gate, turn left alongside a wire
fence on the left and at the next
waymark (39), keep ahead to a
fork.

PUBLIC TRANSPORT None
REFRESHMENTS None
PUBLIC TOILETS None
ORDNANCE SURVEY MAPS Explorer 122 (South Downs Way – Steyning to
Newhaven), Landranger 198 (Brighton & Lewes)

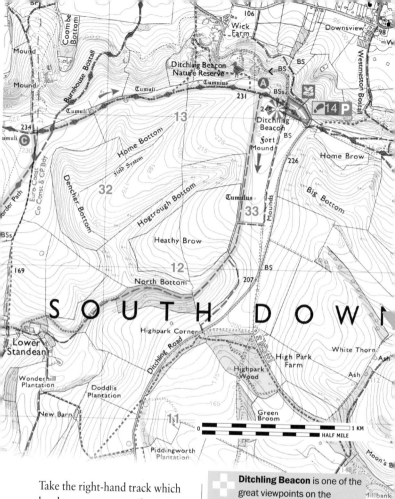

Take the right-hand track which heads up to a gate, go through and continue downhill, curving left to another gate. Go through to a T-junction at Lower Standean, turn

? How high is Ditchling Beacon?

Ditchling Beacon is one of the great viewpoints on the escarpment of the South Downs and its proximity to Brighton and the National Trust car park at its summit make it a popular starting point for walks on the **South Downs Way**. The views across the rolling downs are magnificent and extend northwards across the Weald towards Ashdown Forest.

Down near Ditchling Beacon

right and the track continues steadily uphill to a fork. Take the less obvious, right-hand track – by a fence on the left and following the public bridleway sign – to a gate, go through and turn left along the left edge of a field. Follow the field edge to the right and at a crossways by a finger-post, turn right **B** and

walk across the field to a gate on the far side.

Go through, keep ahead gently uphill to a T-junction and turn right to rejoin the South Downs Way.

C Follow the track, going through several gates, gently uphill to Ditchling Beacon and back to the start. ●

> The walk goes through **North Bottom** and passes by the edge of **Hogtrough** and **Dencher Bottoms**, all examples of dry valleys. Dry valleys are found in chalk and limestone country because the rock is porous and the water seeps through it instead of forming streams.

Bignor – Hill, Roman Villa and Village

START Bignor Hill, National Trust car park, at end of narrow lane about 1½ miles (2.4km) south-west of Bignor village
DISTANCE 4 miles (6.4km)
TIME 2 hours
PARKING Bignor Hill
ROUTE FEATURES Combination of downland, woodland and fields, with some climbing

15

The first part of the route is across Bignor Hill, one of the highest points on the South Downs and a magnificent viewpoint. You then descend through woodland and across fields to the tiny village of Bignor, where there is the chance to visit a medieval church and Roman villa.

Walk back a few yards along the lane and take the track that bears right off it to join the South Downs Way. The track heads over the open downland of Bignor Hill, which rises to 738 ft (225m), and passes to the right of Toby's Stone, a memorial to a local huntsman. It then starts to descend and look out for where it bends sharply to the left Ⓐ and continues more steeply down, bending first right and then left to a finger-post just in front of a barn.

Keep ahead along a track but almost immediately bear left onto a

Although not so great in number as the **mosaics at Fishbourne Palace** (see Walk 19), those at Bignor are equally impressive and rank among the finest in the country. They mostly date from the 4th century. The villa was discovered in 1811 and opened to the public as early as 1814. Apart from the mosaic floors, the baths have been excavated and there is an interesting museum on the site.

path which heads downhill through the lovely woodland of Egg Bottom Coppice. At the bottom, continue along an enclosed track which passes between cottages to a T-junction

PUBLIC TRANSPORT Irregular buses from Chichester, Pulborough and Petworth
REFRESHMENTS None, except for light refreshments at the Roman villa
PUBLIC TOILETS None
ORDNANCE SURVEY MAPS Explorer 121 (Arundel & Pulborough), Landranger 197 (Chichester & the South Downs)

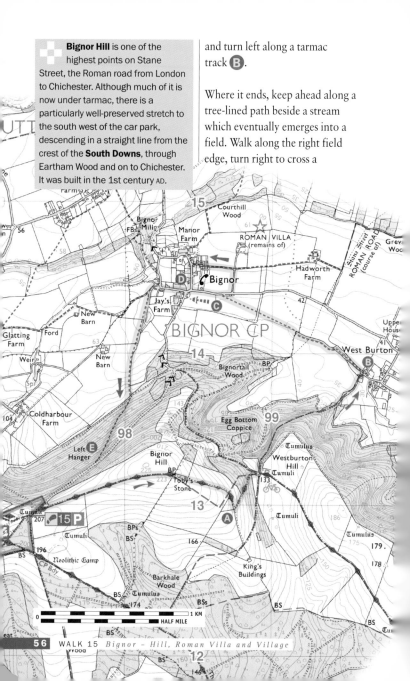

Bignor Hill is one of the highest points on Stane Street, the Roman road from London to Chichester. Although much of it is now under tarmac, there is a particularly well-preserved stretch to the south west of the car park, descending in a straight line from the crest of the **South Downs**, through Eartham Wood and on to Chichester. It was built in the 1st century AD.

and turn left along a tarmac track **B**.

Where it ends, keep ahead along a tree-lined path beside a stream which eventually emerges into a field. Walk along the right field edge, turn right to cross a footbridge and turn left along an enclosed path which continues along the left edge of a field. The path later bears right and heads across the field to a lane **C**.

If not visiting the Roman villa, turn left and rejoin the full walk at point **D**.

For the full walk, turn right along the lane and turn left along a tarmac track to the entrance to the villa. In front of the entrance gates, turn left along an enclosed track and continue between houses and along a tarmac track to a T-junction in Bignor village. On the corner here is a picturesque, timber-framed medieval house with an overhanging thatched roof. The restored medieval church is a short distance to the right.

At the T-junction, turn left along a lane, at the next T-junction turn right **D** and immediately after the lane bends right, turn left, at a public footpath sign, and cross a footbridge over a stream. Bear left along a tree-lined path, by the

A medieval house at Bignor

stream on the left, and at a footpath post, turn left and climb a stile. Walk along the left edge of a field, go through a hedge gap, continue along the left edge of the next field and climb a stile in the corner.

Keep ahead uphill along an enclosed path and on entering the woodland of Left Hanger, turn right along a track. At a finger-post, bear left onto a path which heads steeply uphill through the trees to reach a lane **E** and turn right to continue up to the start. ●

? The signpost in the car park points to Noviomagus. What is the present name of this Roman city?

16 *Beachy Head*

START Beachy Head Countryside Centre
DISTANCE 5¾ miles (9.3km)
TIME 3 hours
PARKING Beachy Head Countryside Centre
ROUTE FEATURES Mostly on grassy tracks and paths across clifftops and over open downland, with some modest climbs

The first part of this exhilarating and highly scenic route is across Beachy Head and there are magnificent views westwards along the coast. You then turn inland for a contrasting walk through the dry valley of Long Down. On the final coastal stretch, there are more fine views, looking eastwards over Eastbourne and Pevensey Bay.

Begin by crossing the road and heading across to the triangulation pillar. Just beyond it, bear right onto a clifftop path. Cross a tarmac path, keep ahead to a former watchtower – a superb viewpoint – and follow the South Downs Way around the headland.

As you follow the curve of the cliffs to the right, magnificent views open up ahead of the disused Belle Tout lighthouse, Birling Gap and the Seven Sisters. Head down into a dip, then up and down again to join a road.

Ⓐ Walk along a grassy path parallel to the road, curving first right and then left, and at a crossways immediately below the Belle Tout lighthouse,

PUBLIC TRANSPORT Buses from Eastbourne
REFRESHMENTS Pub and coffee shop at start
PUBLIC TOILETS At start
ORDNANCE SURVEY MAPS Explorer 123 (South Downs Way – Newhaven to Eastbourne), Landranger 199 (Eastbourne & Hastings)

B turn right down to the road. Cross it and take the concrete track ahead to Cornish Farm – there is a public bridleway sign to Birling Manor. Where the track curves left just before the farm, turn right through a gate.

C Walk along a fence-lined track and go through another gate. The route continues gently uphill, more or less in a straight line, along a track across Long Down for 2 miles (3.2km), passing through a series of gates and finally emerging onto a road on the crest of the down. Cross over, keep ahead, at a public bridleway sign to Beachy Head Road, and from the track there are grand views over Eastbourne and across Pevensey Bay towards Hastings.

D At a finger-post, turn right, in the Birling Gap direction, and at the next one, turn left, in the Seaford direction, and head down towards the sea.

E Look out for the next finger-post where you turn sharp right along a grassy track – now on the South Downs Way again – and head gently uphill onto Beachy Head again. After an enclosed stretch, veer slightly left across the clifftop, then curve right and

The cliffs at **Beachy Head**, the eastern end of the South Downs, are among the highest and most dramatic in England. They are also among the most popular and accessible as they are just a short distance from Eastbourne. The lighthouse on the rocks below was built in 1902 and the disused one at Belle Tout, nearly 2 miles (3.2km) to the west, was erected in 1831. It is fortunate that a huge area of downland to the east of Eastbourne between Beachy Head and **Belle Tout**, around 4000 acres (1620 ha), was bought by the local council in 1929 in order to protect it from development and preserve it as farmland and as an open space for the enjoyment of the public.

continue up towards the Countryside Centre. Finally bear right across the grass to the start. ●

Beachy Head

Midhurst and Cowdray Park

17

START Midhurst
DISTANCE 5¾ miles (9.3km)
TIME 2½ hours
PARKING Midhurst
ROUTE FEATURES Easy walking across fields and through parkland

Much of this walk in the upper Rother valley is across Cowdray Park to the east of Midhurst. There are fine views across the park and valley and historic interest is provided by the ruined mansion of Cowdray and the motte of Midhurst's castle. Allow plenty of time for an exploration of Midhurst, a particularly attractive town.

🖊 The walk starts in Market Square by the church and early 19th-century town hall. Facing the church, turn left along Church Hill, bending left to a T-junction and turn right along North Street.

A Just beyond the tourist information centre, turn right to a public footpath sign to Cowdray Ruins and go through a gate.

Walk along an embankment and cross a bridge over the River Rother.

B In front of the ruined house, turn left along a tarmac drive across Cowdray Park. At a fork, take the right-hand track, keep ahead at a crossways and look out for a footpath post which directs you to turn right along a track to a stile. Climb it, continue by a fence on the right, climb another stile, keep ahead and at a fence corner, bear slightly right across a field to a stile. After climbing it, head gently uphill across the next field to emerge, via a kissing-gate, onto the busy A272.

❓ *Name any two sports played in Cowdray Park.*

PUBLIC TRANSPORT Buses from Worthing, Petersfield, Chichester and Haslemere
REFRESHMENTS Pubs and cafés at Midhurst
PUBLIC TOILETS Midhurst
ORDNANCE SURVEY MAPS Explorer 133 (Haslemere & Petersfield), Landranger 197 (Chichester & the South Downs)

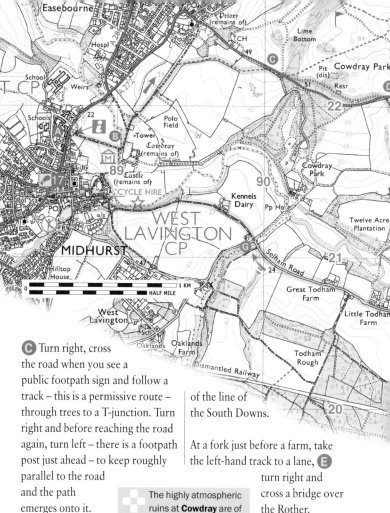

C Turn right, cross the road when you see a public footpath sign and follow a track – this is a permissive route – through trees to a T-junction. Turn right and before reaching the road again, turn left – there is a footpath post just ahead – to keep roughly parallel to the road and the path emerges onto it.

D Cross over and at a public footpath sign, take the tarmac path to Moor Farm. Ahead there is a fine view

The highly atmospheric ruins at **Cowdray** are of a great Tudor mansion, built by the **Earl of Southampton** and begun in 1530. A fire in 1793 left it roofless and uninhabitable and it has been a ruin ever since. The remains of the gatehouse are particularly impressive.

of the line of the South Downs.

At a fork just before a farm, take the left-hand track to a lane, **E** turn right and cross a bridge over the Rother. Immediately turn right through a gate, at a public footpath sign, and walk across a field, heading up to climb a stile at the

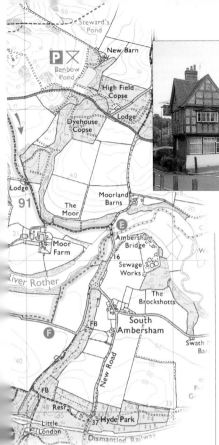

Buildings at Midhurst

After passing through gates, keep ahead along an enclosed track, go through a gate and continue along a path by the left inside edge of woodland. The path descends to a T-junction. Turn right, cross a bridge in front of a wooded hill – this is the motte of a former castle – turn left and head uphill, curving right to a gate at the top. Go through and walk along a lane (St Annes Hill) to return to the start. ●

Midhurst has buildings of all ages lining its streets and small squares. The number of fine old coaching inns is an indication that it was once an important staging post on the road from London to Chichester. Of the Norman castle, which occupied a commanding position above the River Rother, only earthworks survive. This is passed at the end of the walk. The mainly 15th-century church was once a chapel of nearby **Easebourne Priory**. It was restored by the Victorians. **H.G. Wells** lived for a while in the town.

far tapering end. Turn right along a narrow enclosed path above the river – this may well be overgrown – and the path later continues across a field to a lane.

F Turn right along this narrow lane and after almost 1 mile (1.6km) – where the lane bends left – keep ahead along the tarmac track to Kennels Dairy **G**.

● Site of battle ● woodland ● ruined abbey ● medieval church

18 *Around Battle*

START Battle

DISTANCE 5 miles (8km)
Shorter version 3½ miles
(5.6km)

TIME 2½ hours (1½ hours
for shorter walk)

PARKING Battle

ROUTE FEATURES An
undulating route across
fields, through woodland
and along roads

*This undulating walk has great historic
interest as it traverses part of the site of
what is generally regarded as the most
significant battle in English history and
there are views of the battlefield and of
Battle Abbey from various points. The
shorter version returns directly to the town; the full walk
takes you through the attractive Great Wood to the east of it.*

Facing the abbey gateway,
turn right along a lane and where it
ends at a car park, keep ahead, at a
public bridleway sign, along an
enclosed track. Go through a gate
and continue gently downhill along
the left edge of a field which
borders Saxon Wood.

A At a fork by a footpath post,
take the left-hand path which
keeps by the right edge of the
wood and then continues downhill
to a stile. Climb it, keep ahead
along an enclosed track, pass
through a belt of trees, climb

another stile and continue gently
uphill. Climb a stile onto a track,
climb the stile opposite and the
path bends right to keep along the
right edge of a field, parallel to a
road below on the left.

After climbing the next stile, keep
ahead to the road, **B** cross
carefully – there is an awkward
bend – and take the lane opposite

*Why is the site of the high
altar at Battle Abbey
particularly significant?*

PUBLIC TRANSPORT Buses from all surrounding towns, trains from Tunbridge
Wells and Hastings
REFRESHMENTS Pubs and cafés at Battle
PUBLIC TOILETS Battle
ORDNANCE SURVEY MAPS Explorer 124 (Hastings & Bexhill), Landranger 199
(Eastbourne & Hastings)

(Telham Lane). Keep along it for about 1 ¼ miles (2km) – Battle Abbey can be seen on the hilltop to the left – and just before the lane curves right, turn left over a stile, at a public footpath sign **C**.

Head downhill across a field towards trees, making for a telegraph pole, and continue past it down to a stile. Climb it, continue through a belt of trees, cross a stream, head

uphill and on emerging from the trees, bear right.

Follow a track gently uphill across a field towards the next woodland, continue through the wood, climb a stile at the far end and keep ahead along an enclosed path to another stile. Climb that one, continue along a hedge- and tree-lined path, climb a stile and keep ahead to a track and onto a road 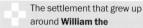 **D**.

The settlement that grew up around **William the Conqueror's** foundation is now an attractive and bustling town, with some fine old buildings and a good selection of shops, cafés, pubs and restaurants to cater for its many visitors. Of particular interest is the impressive Norman church, founded by one of the abbots of Battle in the early-12th century.

Turn left if doing the short walk and the road leads back to the start.

Battle Abbey

The site of the Battle of Hastings

For the full walk, turn right uphill and in front of a cottage – and by a 40mph sign – bear left along a track (Starrs Green Lane). At a T-junction, bear left and at a public footpath sign, turn left along an enclosed path **E**. Pass beside a barrier, keep ahead along a tree- and hedge-lined path and at a fork, take the right-hand path to continue through Great Wood. Bear left on joining a broad, straight track, follow it to a crossways and turn left along another wide track **F**.

The track narrows to a path and continues to a road. Bear left, head uphill, go over a level-crossing and keep ahead to a T-junction. Turn right, passing Battle church, to return to the start.

On 14 October **1066** the best-known battle in English history was fought on a hill about 7 miles (11.3km) to the north of Hastings. Before the crucial encounter, **William the Conqueror** vowed that if he won, he would show his gratitude to God by building an abbey on the site. Of this great abbey, little of the church is left and some of the buildings are used as a school – and not open to the public – but the impressive 14th-century gatehouse and fine dormitory range remain. The battlefield slopes away to the south of the abbey buildings and well-signed Battlefield Trails guide you around the site.

19 Bosham and Fishbourne

START Bosham

DISTANCE 6½ miles (10.5km) Shorter version 6 miles (9.7km)

TIME 3 hours (2½ hours for shorter walk)

PARKING Bosham

ROUTE FEATURES Mostly along tracks and field paths across the flat country around Chichester Harbour

There is plenty of historic interest, as well as wide views and fresh breezes, on this flat walk across pasture and marshland fringing the creeks and inlets of Chichester Harbour. The walk starts in the delightful village of Bosham, with its Saxon church and picturesque quayside, and passes close to the remains of the Roman palace at Fishbourne, renowned for its outstanding mosaics and well worth a short detour.

From the car park, take the lane signposted to Harbour and Village and at a T-junction, turn left to the quay. Just before the next T-junction, turn left onto a tarmac path between houses. The path, raised above the shore and parallel lane – the lane is flooded every tide – curves right and just before it meets a lane, turn left along the left edge of a grassy area. Cross a lane to a public footpath sign and keep ahead along an enclosed path to a lane **A**. Cross over, climb steps and continue across a field. On the far side, cross a drainage channel, turn right to cross a ditch and at a public footpath sign, turn left along a track. Later the route continues along a

PUBLIC TRANSPORT Buses from Chichester

REFRESHMENTS Pubs and cafés at Bosham, pubs at Fishbourne, café at Fishbourne Roman Palace

PUBLIC TOILETS At start

ORDNANCE SURVEY MAPS Explorer 120 (Chichester), Landranger 197 (Chichester & the South Downs)

path in front of a cottage and then along the left edge of a field. After going through a hedge gap, keep ahead along an enclosed path and pass beside a barrier onto a lane.

Cross over and as you continue across fields, fine views open up of the spire of Chichester Cathedral and the line of the South Downs. The path later becomes enclosed and at a T-junction, turn right **B** along a broad, grassy track. At a

The small village of **Bosham,** an important port in Saxon and medieval times, is now a popular boating centre and its picturesque cottages stretch along an inlet of **Chichester Harbour**, surrounded by water and marsh. At the top of the narrow High Street is the delightful grassy area of Quay Meadow, overlooked by the ancient church. Much of the church – including the tower, walls of the nave and superb chancel arch – is Saxon. It has the distinction of appearing in the Bayeux Tapestry as it was from Bosham that the future King Harold, then Earl of Wessex, sailed on his ill-fated trip to Normandy in 1064.

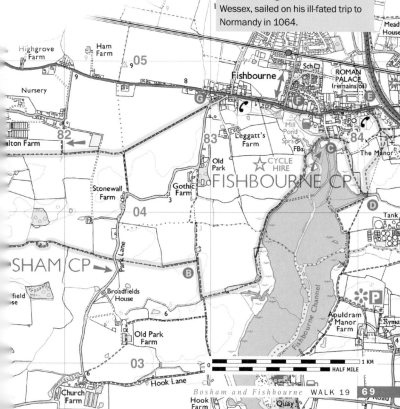

public footpath sign, turn left along another broad track by the right edge of a field, keep ahead between scrub and continue across marshland. After the path curves left to pass through a small group of trees, it keeps beside an inlet. Look out for where you bear left up steps to go through a hedge gap and continue first along an enclosed path and then along the top of the sea wall.

Turn right down steps to descend from the embankment, continue between tall grass, crossing several footbridges, and finally keep along the right edge of a mill pond to emerge onto the end of a lane.

 Cross over, go through a kissing-gate, at a public footpath sign to Fishbourne church, and walk along a path, by a stream on the left. After going through another kissing-gate, the route continues along a boardwalk across Fishbourne Meadows, once part of a Roman harbour linked to the palace but later reclaimed. Cross a footbridge over a stream, go through a kissing-gate, continue along a path, climb steps, pass through a fence gap and keep ahead above a creek.

 At a public footpath sign at the head of the creek, turn left over a stile, walk across a field and climb a stile on the far side. Keep ahead across the next field and in the corner, climb a stile and go through

Bosham

a kissing-gate into the churchyard of Fishbourne church. This picturesque building is on a medieval site but was mainly rebuilt in the Victorian era. Keep ahead to a tarmac path, turn sharp left, go through a kissing-gate in the corner of the churchyard and continue in the same direction across a meadow to another kissing-gate. Go through, walk along a tree-lined path, and pass through a kissing-gate onto a main road **E**.

Turn left through Fishbourne. If doing the full walk, which takes in the Roman palace, turn right along Salthill Road **F** and right again along Roman Way to the entrance. *For the short walk, simply continue along the main road and pick up the route directions in the next paragraph.*

From the Roman palace, retrace your steps to the main road **F**, turn right and turn left along Old Park Lane. Where it bears left, keep ahead along a track **G**.

At a public footpath sign pass beside a gate, keep by a left field

> **?** *The daughter of a King of England is allegedly buried in Bosham church. Which King?*

The Roman palace at **Fishbourne** was accidentally discovered in 1960 by local water board workmen while digging a trench. The palace, the largest Roman building in Britain and one of the largest in the empire outside Rome, is thought to have belonged to **Tiberius Claudius Cogidubunus**, a local British chief, who co-operated with the conquerors. This huge and sumptuous palace was probably his reward. It was built in the 1st century AD but much of it lies under the A259 and the buildings of the present village of Fishbourne. The most fully excavated part, the north wing, is covered by a modern building to protect the finest display of Roman mosaics in the country. Outside, the Roman garden has been replanted on its original lines.

edge and after passing a public footpath sign, the route continues along an enclosed track. Cross a track and keep ahead along field edges to emerge onto a road at a bend.

Keep ahead into Bosham and opposite the Berkeley Arms, turn left along an enclosed tarmac path. Cross a road, keep ahead to emerge onto a road, continue ahead and turn right along Harbour Road. Where it ends, keep ahead along a tarmac path to a T-junction and turn right. Here you pick up the outward route and retrace your steps to the start. ●

20 *Ashdown Forest*

START Gills Lap car park, at junction of B2026 (to Hartfield) and minor road to Forest Row

DISTANCE 5½ miles (8.9km)

TIME 3 hours

PARKING Gills Lap

ROUTE FEATURES Open heathland and woodland, some steady climbing

Initially the walk descends from the open heathland – and superb viewpoint – of Gills Lap and continues through woodland to Pooh Bridge. A steady climb through the beautiful Five Hundred Acre Wood leads to Greenwood Gate Clump, at 723 ft (223m) the highest point in Ashdown Forest, and this is followed by a final stretch across heathland.

Pooh Bridge, Ashdown Forest

At a height of 679 ft (207m), there are superb views over the Weald right from the start. Facing the information board in the car park, take the broad track that passes to the right of it. The track passes to the left of a triangulation pillar and to the right of a memorial and descends across the open heathland. Keep on the main track all the while and at the bottom, it bends right to emerge onto a lane.

Ⓐ Turn left and take the first lane on the right. Just after it curves left, turn right, Ⓑ at a public footpath

PUBLIC TRANSPORT None

REFRESHMENTS None

PUBLIC TOILETS None

ORDNANCE SURVEY MAPS Explorer 135 (Ashdown Forest), Landrangers 198 (Brighton & Lewes) and 199 (Eastbourne & Hastings)

A.A. Milne, author of the popular *Winnie the Pooh* books, lived near Hartfield in Ashdown Forest and the local area is the setting for many of the stories. A shop in Hartfield called Pooh Corner has a large selection of gifts and memorabilia. The walk passes through Five Hundred Acre Wood, the One Hundred Acre Wood in the books, and takes you to Pooh Bridge, a delightful spot in Posingford Wood where Winnie the Pooh and his friends played '**Pooh-sticks**', droppng sticks into the stream and seeing which was the first to float under the bridge.

stone and a sign to Pooh Bridge, and head downhill along the left

inside edge of Posingford Wood to Pooh Bridge, a delightful part of the walk **C**.

Retrace your steps to the lane **B** and where it curves right, leave the previous route by keeping ahead, at a public footpath stone, along a path through trees.

D After about 200 yds (183m), look out for a path on the left which leads to a stile on the edge of the wood. Climb the stile and walk across a field, heading down to a stile in the corner. Climb it, follow a path through another part of Posingford Wood, climb another

Memorial to A.A. Milne, Ashdown Forest

Who collaborated with A.A. Milne on the Winnie the Pooh **books?**

stile on the far side of the trees and walk along the left edge of a field.

Follow the field edge to the right and in the top corner, climb a stile, cross a track and climb another stile. Cross a gallop, go through a gate, keep ahead across a paddock and on the far side, go through another gate and cross the gallop again. Keep ahead over a stile and on through trees to a road and turn left.

E At a public footpath stone, turn right along a sunken path which heads downhill through Five Hundred Acre Wood.

Cross a footbridge over a stream, keep ahead to a finger-post and turn sharp right, here joining the Wealdway **F**.

Head steadily uphill through the wood – keeping on the main path all the while – go through a gate, continue uphill and look out for a fork where a Wealdway post directs you to take the right-hand path. Continue steadily up eventually to emerge from the wood onto open heathland and keep ahead to reach Greenwood Gate Clump, a prominent circle of trees. At 723 ft (223m), this is the highest point in Ashdown Forest and a magnificent viewpoint.

At a fork, take the right-hand track **G** – here leaving the Wealdway – and at the next fork, take the right-hand track again. Follow it across the heathland and the track curves gradually right to return to the start.

Ashdown Forest comprises around 6000 acres (2430 ha) of elevated heathland, covered with gorse, bracken and heather and dotted with pines and birches. There is thicker woodland on the lower slopes and in the valleys. It was once part of the vast ancient forest of Andredesweald that stretched from Kent, across Surrey and Sussex into Hampshire, and it originally covered an area of around 18,000 acres (7290 ha) between Tunbridge Wells, East Grinstead and Lewes. As with the other Wealden forests, its woodlands were felled to meet the demands for timber from both the local iron industry and the Navy and it became considerably reduced in size. Regular conflicts between the owners, who wanted to enclose it, and local people, who wished to keep their common rights, were finally settled in the 19th century and, since 1885, the forest has been administered by a board of conservators and maintained as an open access area.

Further Information

Walking Safety

Always take with you both warm and waterproof clothing and sufficient food and drink. Wear suitable footwear, i.e. strong walking boots or shoes that give a good grip over stony ground, on slippery slopes and in muddy conditions. Try to obtain a local weather forecast and bear it in mind before you start. Do not be afraid to abandon your proposed route and return to your starting point in the event of a sudden and unexpected deterioration in the weather.

All the walks described in this book will be safe to do, given due care and respect, even during the winter. Indeed, a crisp, fine winter day often provides perfect walking conditions, with firm ground underfoot and a clarity of light unique to that time of the year.

The most difficult hazard likely to be encountered is mud, especially when walking along woodland and field paths, farm tracks and bridleways – the latter in particular can often get churned up by cyclists and horses. In summer, an additional difficulty may be narrow and overgrown paths, particularly along the edges of cultivated fields. Neither should constitute a major problem provided that the appropriate footwear is worn.

Follow the Country Code

- Enjoy the countryside and respect its life and work
- Guard against all risk of fire
- Take your litter home
- Fasten all gates
- Help to keep all water clean
- Keep your dogs under control
- Protect wildlife, plants and trees
- Keep to public paths across farmland
- Take special care on country roads
- Leave livestock, crops and machinery alone
- Make no unnecessary noise
- Use gates and stiles to cross fences, hedges and walls
            (The Countryside Agency)

Useful Organisations

Council for the Protection of Rural England
128 Southwark St,
London SE1 0SW.
Tel. 020 798 12800

Strand Gate, Winchelsea

Countryside Agency
246 Lavender Hill,
London SW11 1LJ.
Tel. 020 792 44077

East Sussex County Council
County Hall, St Anne's Crescent,
Lewes, East Sussex BN7 1UN.
Tel. 01273 481000

Forestry Commission
Information Branch,
231 Corstorphine Road,
Edinburgh EH12 7AT.
Tel. 0131 334 0303

**Southeastern England Forest
Enterprise**
Bucks Horn Oak,
Farnham, Surrey GU10 4LS.

Tel. 01420 23666; Fax 01420
22082

National Trust
Membership and general enquiries:
PO Box 39, Bromley,
Kent BR1 3XL.
Tel. 020 8315 1111
E-mail: enquiries@ntrust.org.uk

*Kent and East Sussex Regional
Office:*
The Estate Office, Scotney Castle,
Lamberhurst, Tunbridge Wells,
Kent TN3 8JN.
Tel. 01892 890651; Fax 01892
890110
Southern Regional Office:
Polesden Lacey, Dorking,
Surrey RH5 6BD.

Tel. 01372 453401; Fax 01372 452023

Ordnance Survey
Romsey Road, Maybush,
Southampton SO16 4GU.
Tel. 08456 05 05 05 (Lo-call)
www.ordnancesurvey.co.uk

Ramblers' Association
2nd Floor, Camelford House,
87–90 Albert Embankment,
London SE1 7TW.
Tel. 020 7339 8500

Youth Hostels Association
Trevelyan House, Dimple Road,
Matlock, Derbyshire DE4 3YH.

Tel. 01629 592600
Website: www.yha.org.uk

English Heritage
23 Savile Row, London W1X 1AB.
Tel. 0171 973 3250;
Fax 0171 973 3146;
www.english-heritage.org.uk

English Nature
Northminster House,
Peterborough PE1 1UA.
Tel. 01733 455100;
Fax 01733 455103; E-mail
enquiries@english-nature.org.uk;
www.english-nature.org.uk

Near Bignor

Local Organisations

West Sussex County Council
County Hall, Chichester
West Sussex PO19 1RQ.
Tel. 01243 777100
County Planning,
Tourism: 01903 777488;
e-mail: tourism@westsussex.gov.uk

East Sussex County Council
County Hall, St Anne's Crescent,
Lewes, East Sussex, BN7 1UN.
Tel. 01273 481000

Southeastern England Forest Enterprise
Bucks Horn Oak, Farnham, Surrey
GU10 4LS.
Tel. 01420 23666

South East England Tourist Board
The Old Brew House,
Warwick Park,
Tunbridge Wells, Kent TN2 5TU
Tel. 01892 540766

Local Tourist Information Centres

Call 0870 40022300 to connect to
any TIC in the UK

Arundel: 01903 882268
Battle: 01424 773721
Bexhill-on-Sea: 01424 732208
Bognor Regis: 01243 823140
Brighton & Hove: 0906 711 2255
(50p/min)

Chichester: 01243 775888
Eastbourne: 01323 411400
Hastings: 01424 781111
Horsham: 01403 211661
Lewes: 01273 483448
Littlehampton: 01903 713480
Midhurst: 01730 817322/815933
Rye: 01797 226696
Seaford: 01323 897426
Worthing: 01903 210022

Public Transport

For all public transport enquiries:
Traveline: 0870 608 2608

Ordnance Survey Maps

Explorer maps: 120 (Chichester),
121 (Arundel & Pulborough), 122
(South Downs Way – Steyning to
Newhaven), 123 (South Downs
Way – Newhaven to Eastbourne),
124 (Hastings & Bexhill), 133
(Haslemere & Petersfield), 135
(Ashdown Forest), 136 (The Weald).
Landranger maps: 189 (Ashford &
Romney Marsh), 197 (Chichester
& the South Downs), 198
(Brighton & Lewes) and 199
(Eastbourne & Hastings).

Answers to Questions

Walk 1: 800 years.
Walk 2: Pipewell Gate.
Walk 3: 2 shillings (10 pence).
Walk 4: 1698 – the date can be
seen in front of the building.
Walk 5: Sir Edward Dalyngrigge.

Walk 6: Meanders.

Walk 7: The village it served has vanished because, from the 14th century onwards, the river began to silt up, trade along it ceased and the people moved away.

Walk 8: It is now an International Study Centre for a Canadian university – Queens University, Kingston, Ontario.

Walk 9: To look after and generally keep a close watch on a stretch of coastline.

Walk 10: 15,908 million.

Walk 11: 13th century.

Walk 12: Beech.

Walk 13: South Harting.

Walk 14: 814 ft (248m).

Walk 15: Chichester.

Walk 16: Chalk.

Walk 17: Polo, cricket, golf.

Walk 18: This is where, it is alleged, King Harold was killed during the Battle of Hastings.

Walk 19: Canute.

Walk 20: E.H. Shepard – it tells you on the memorial just after the start of the walk.